Coloring the World of Felines: Children's Activity Book!

Welcome to the wonderful world of kittens in this charming coloring book for children. This book is perfect for little artists who love cats and enjoy expressing themselves through colors.

Filled with adorable drawings of cats of all kinds, each page offers an artistic adventure. This book has been carefully created to stimulate creativity and provide hours of colorful fun.

The kittens in this book are ready to come to life with vibrant and cheerful colors. Let children's imagination soar as they fill each page with unique shades and patterns.

Ideal for children aged 4 to 11, "the World of Felines" is the perfect companion for creative afternoons and moments of relaxation. Grab your colored pencils and join us on this feline artistic journey!

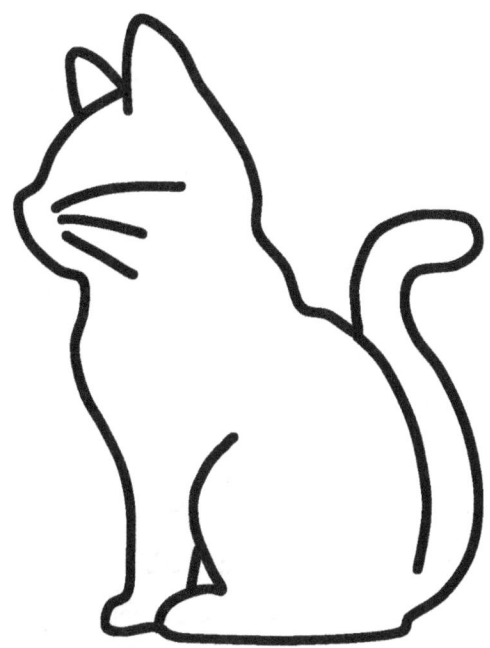

Danny Lima
2024

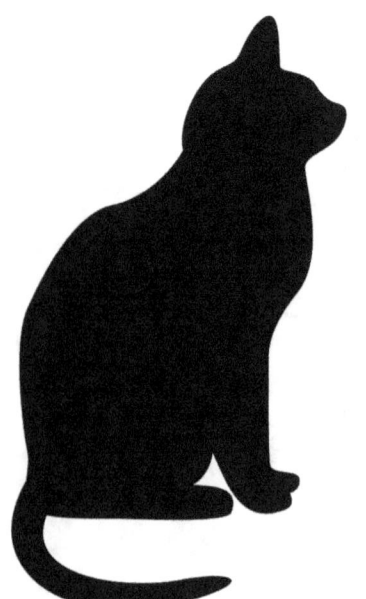

This Book Belongs to:

○_____○

D.L.P.©

Danny Lima publications

ALL RIGHTS RESERVED©
2024

No part of this publication may be reproduced, distributed, or transmitted in any form or by any means, including photocopying, recording, or other electronic or mechanical methods, without the prior written permission of the publisher, except for brief quotations incorporated in critical reviews and other specific noncommercial uses. Any unauthorized replica of this work is prohibited.

D.L. P©

Danny Lima publications

Test Color Page

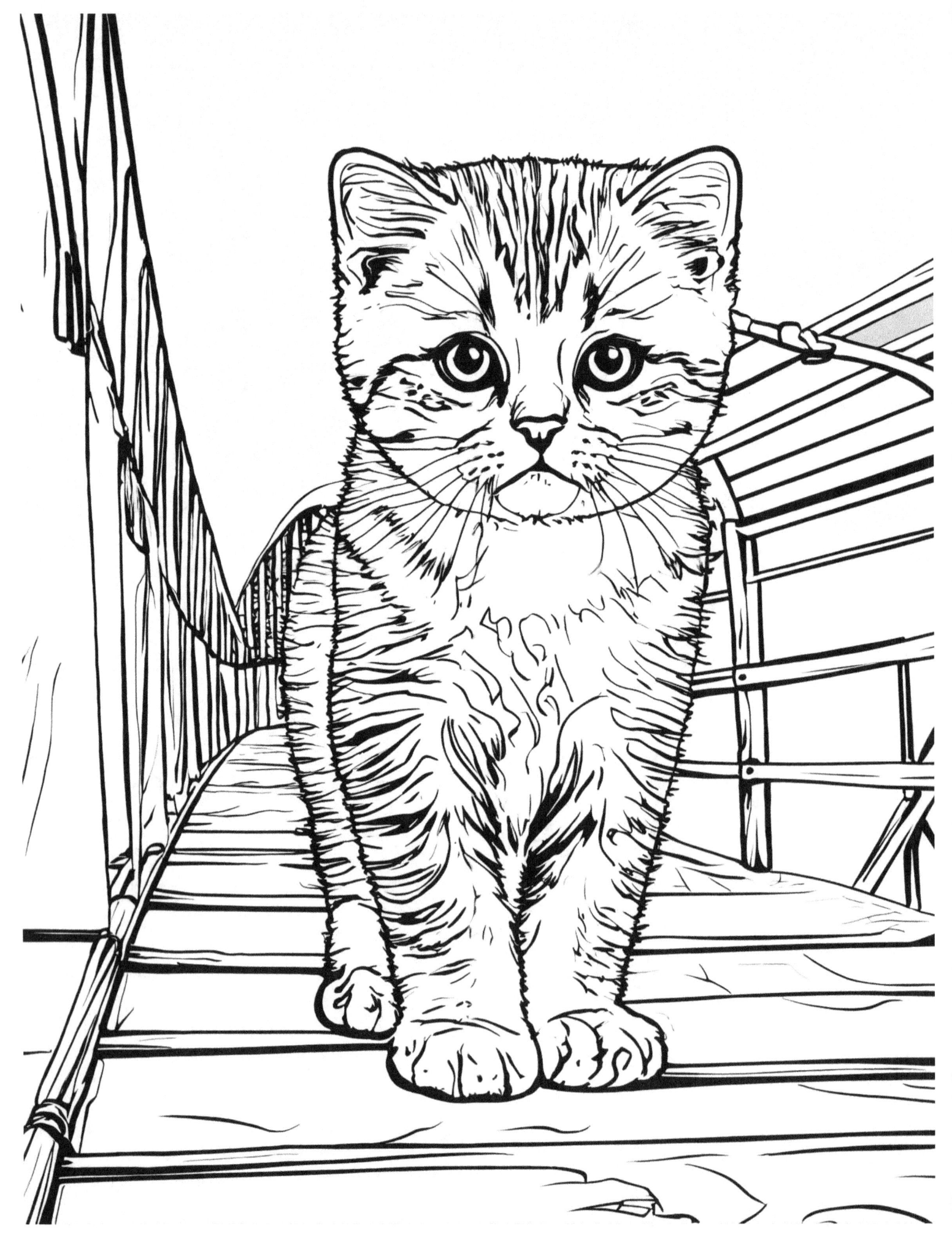

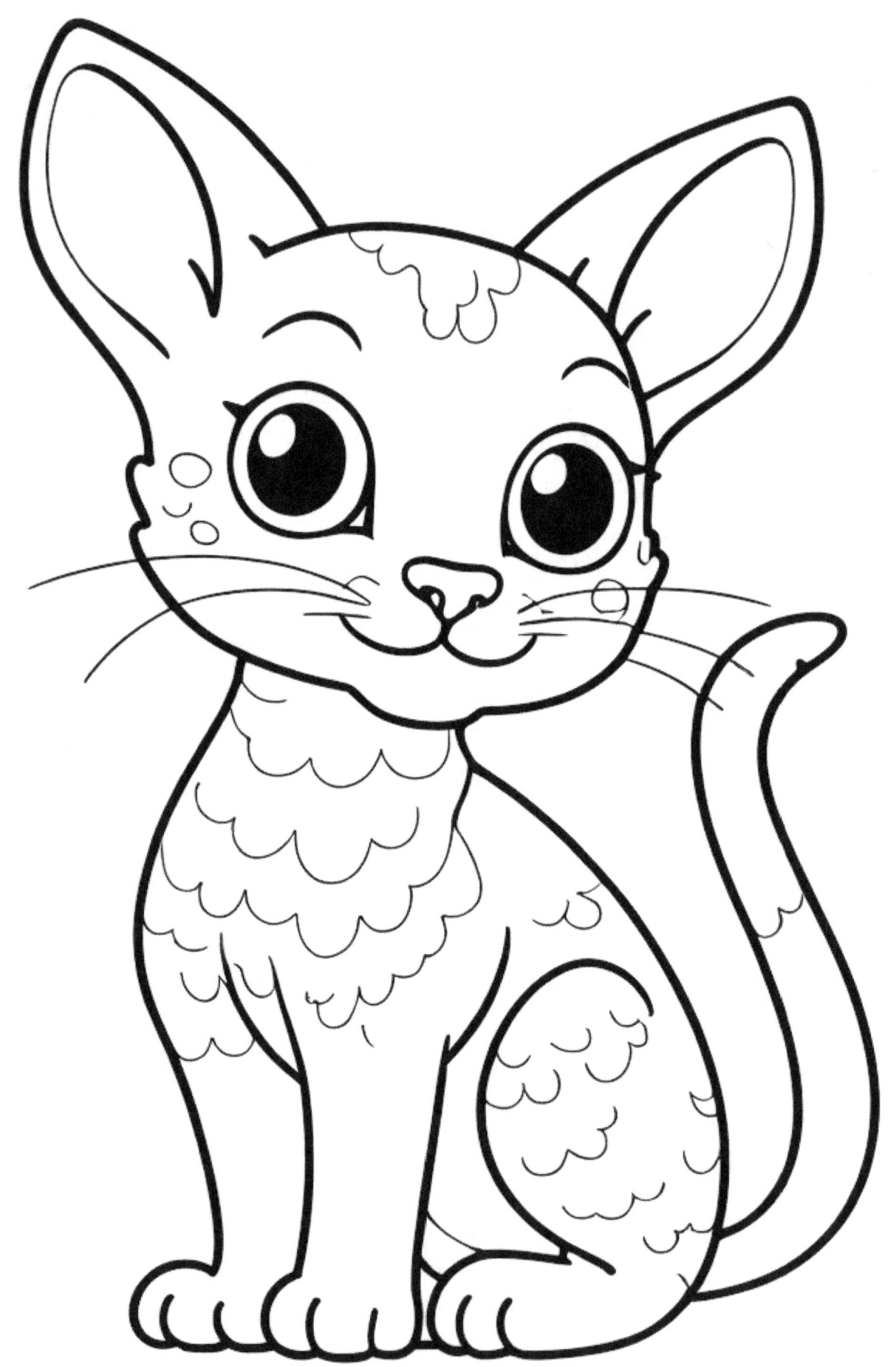

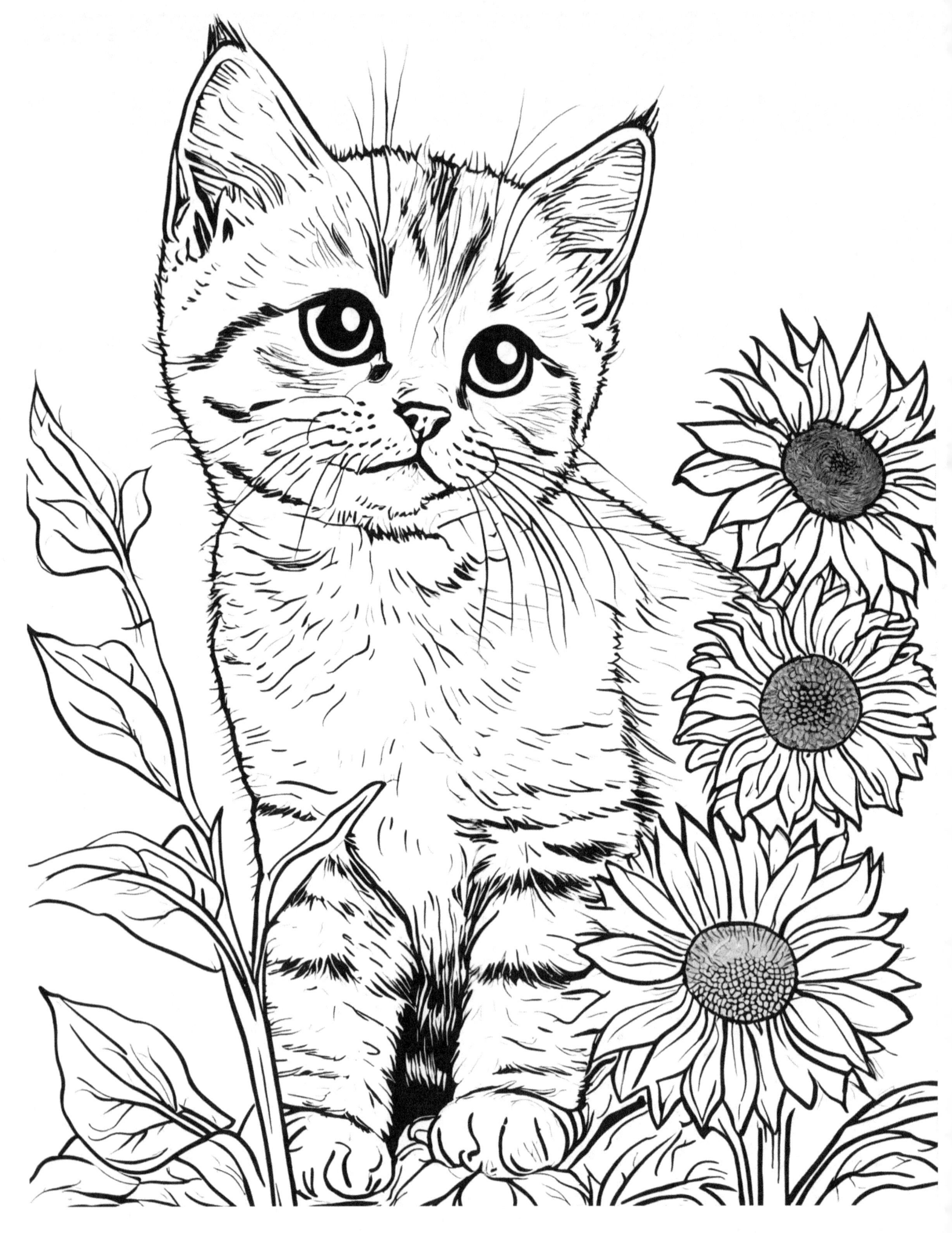

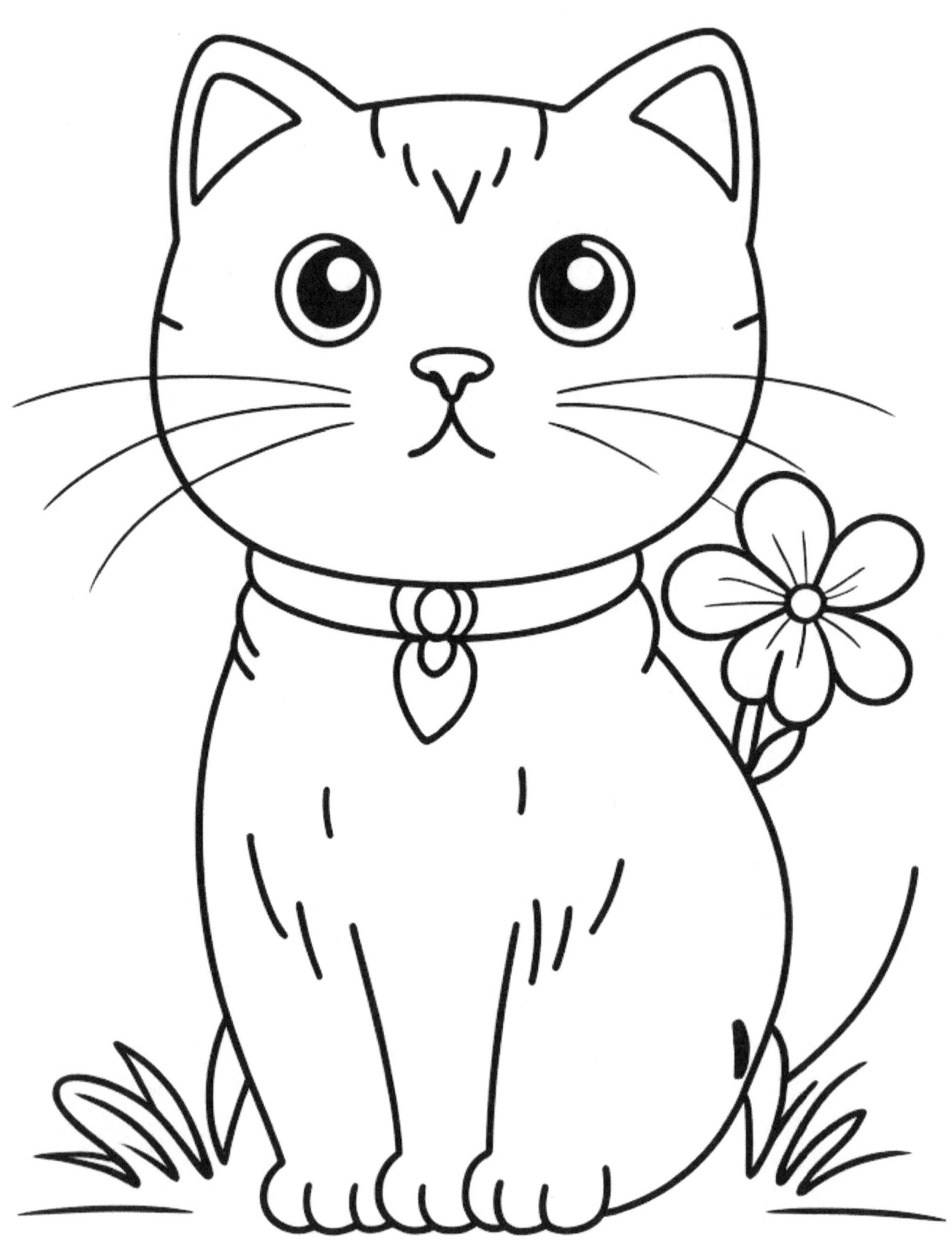

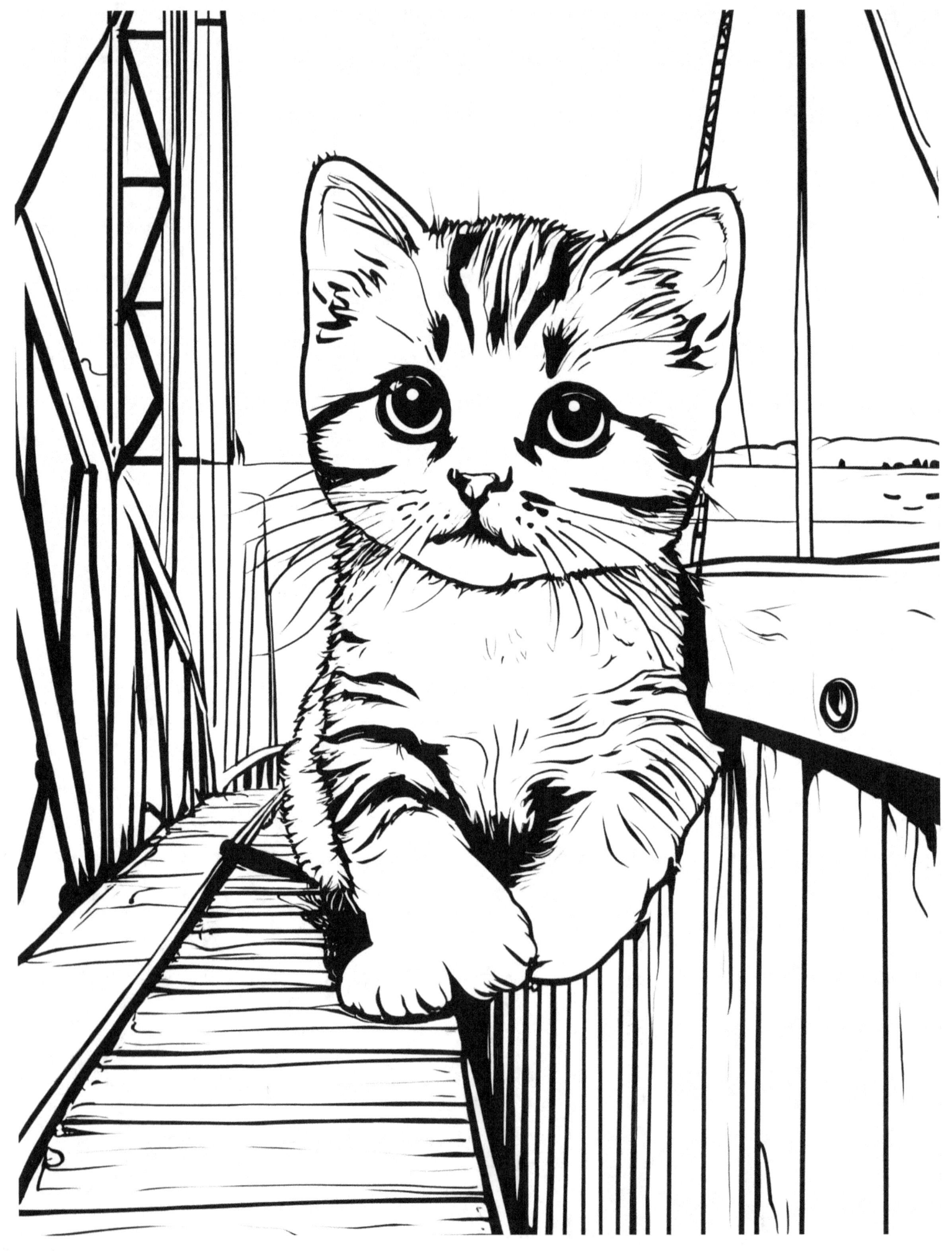

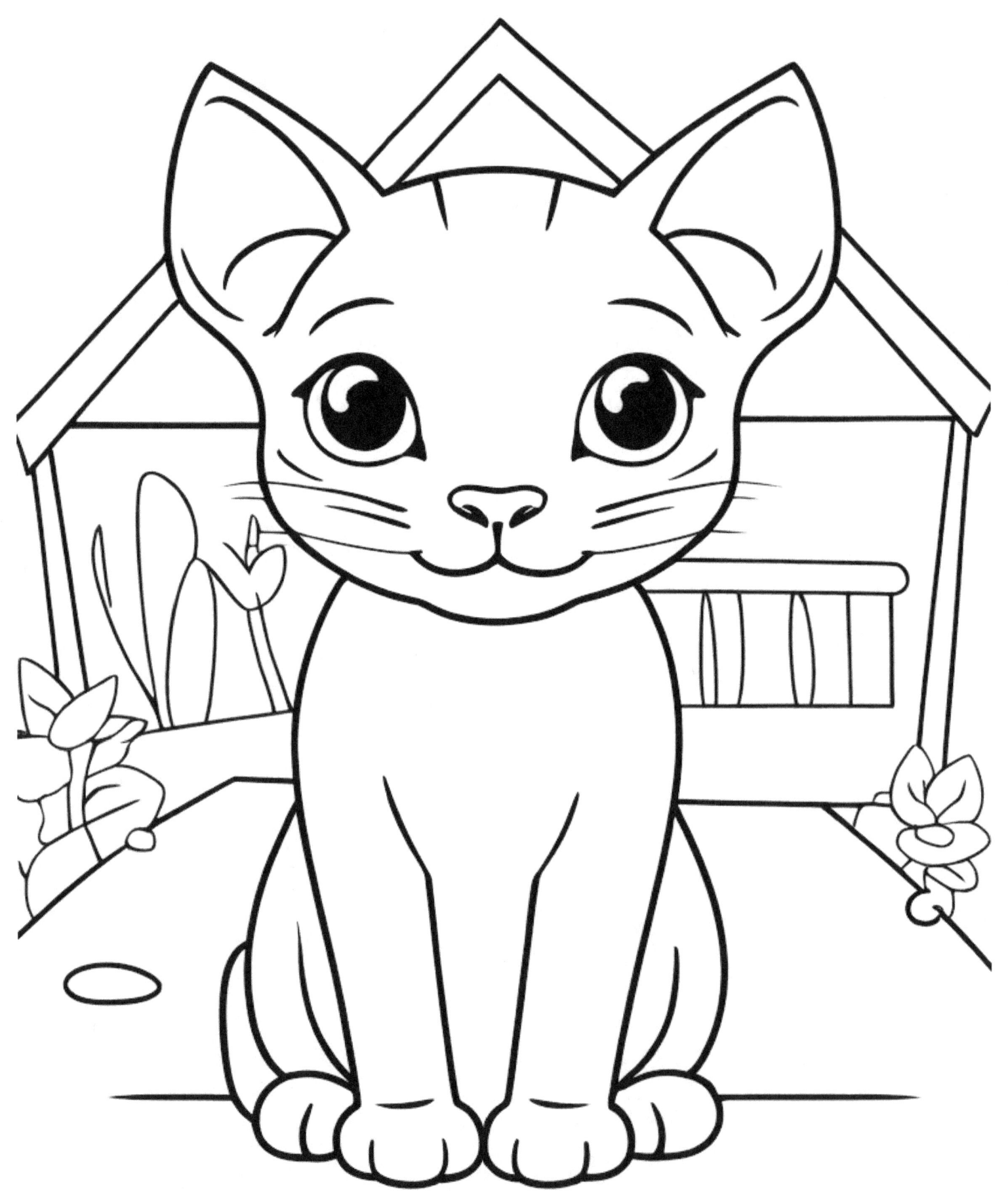

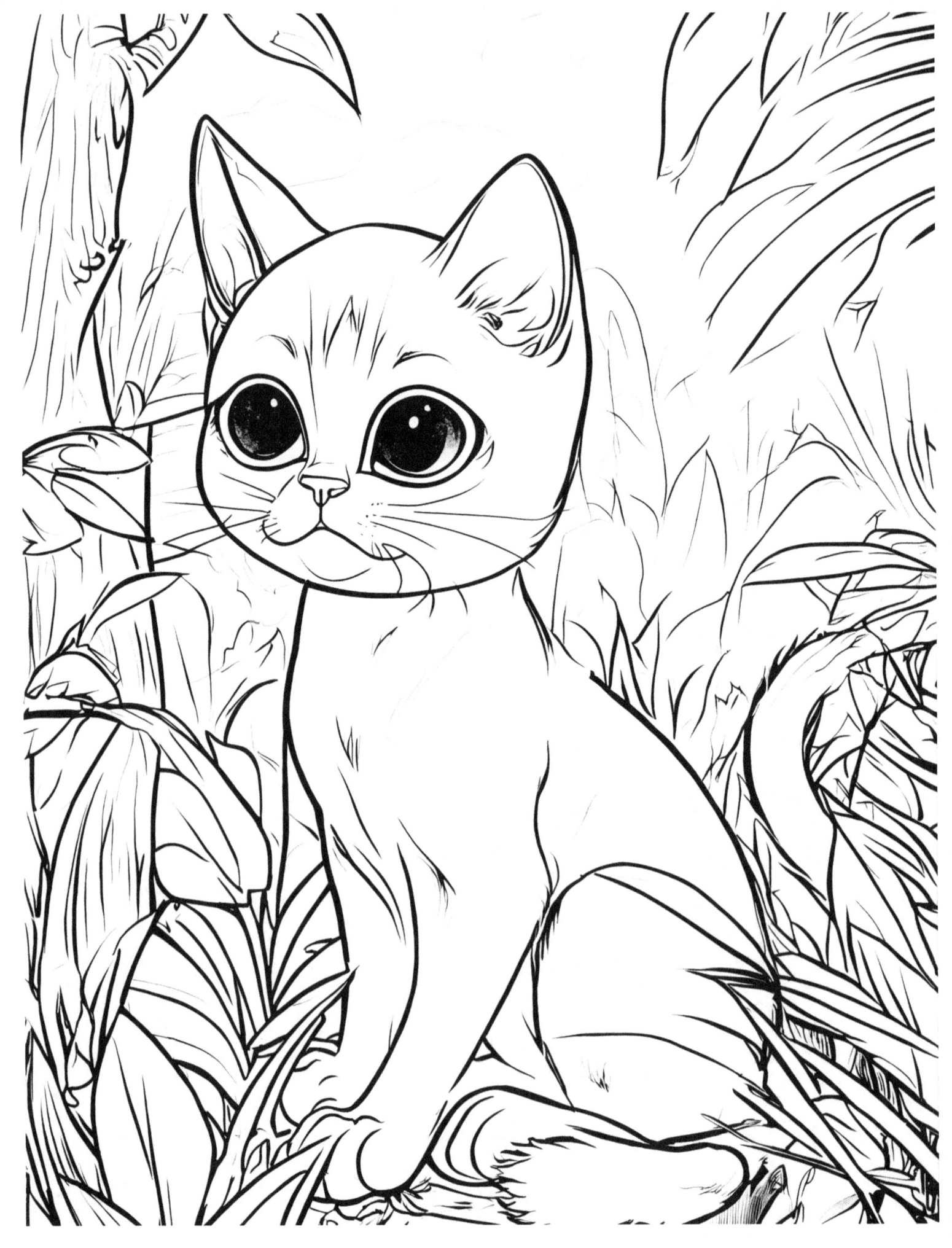

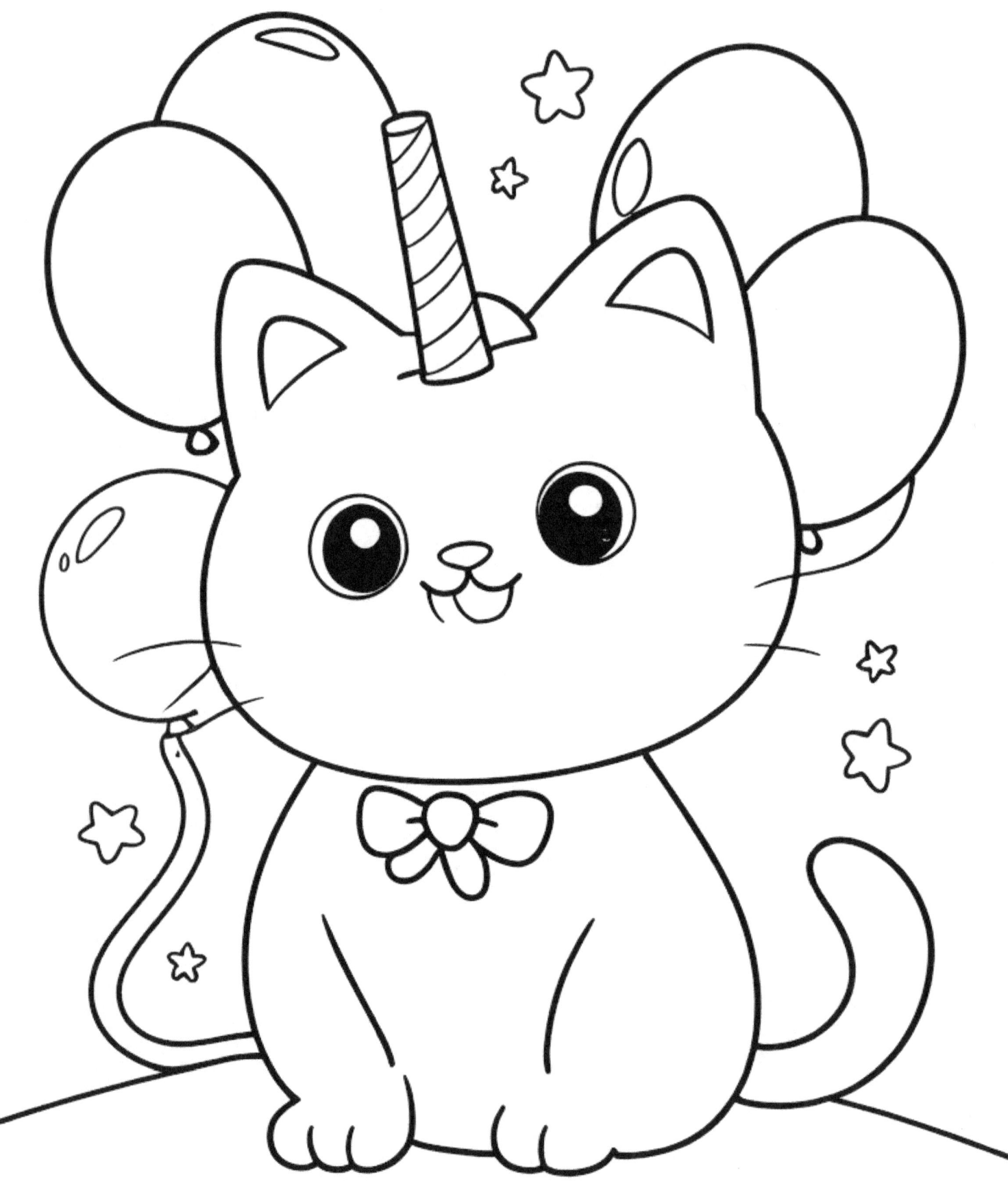

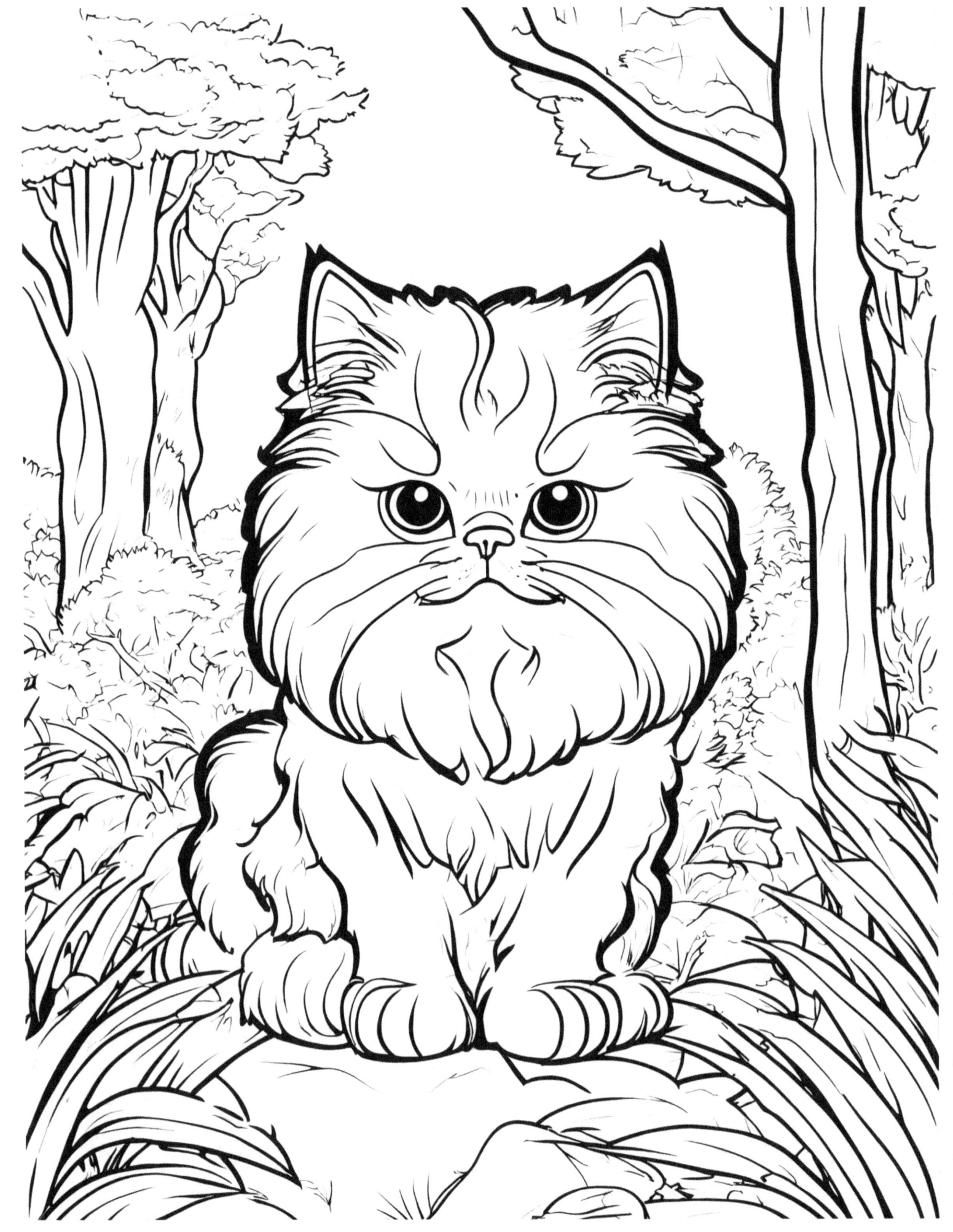

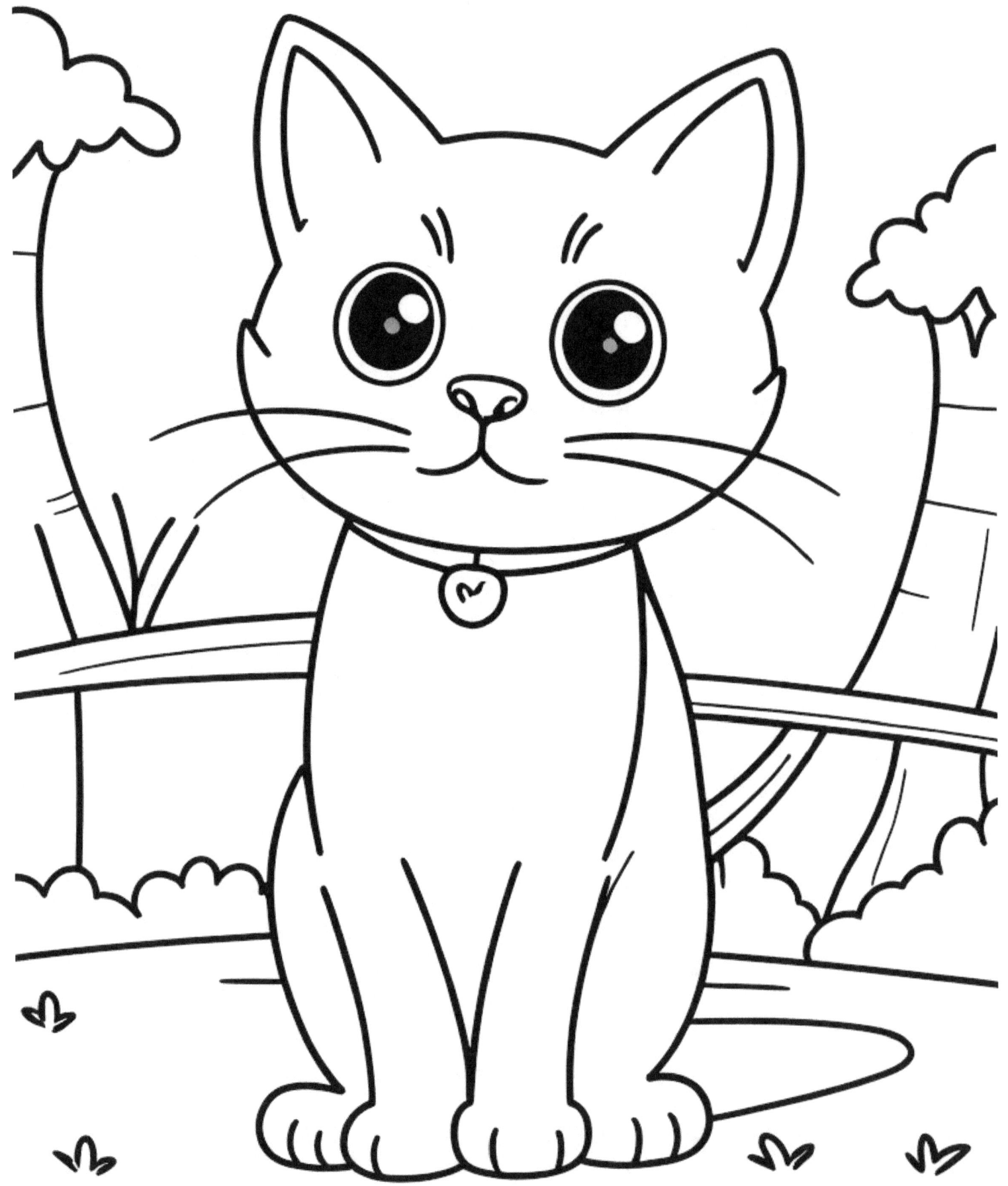

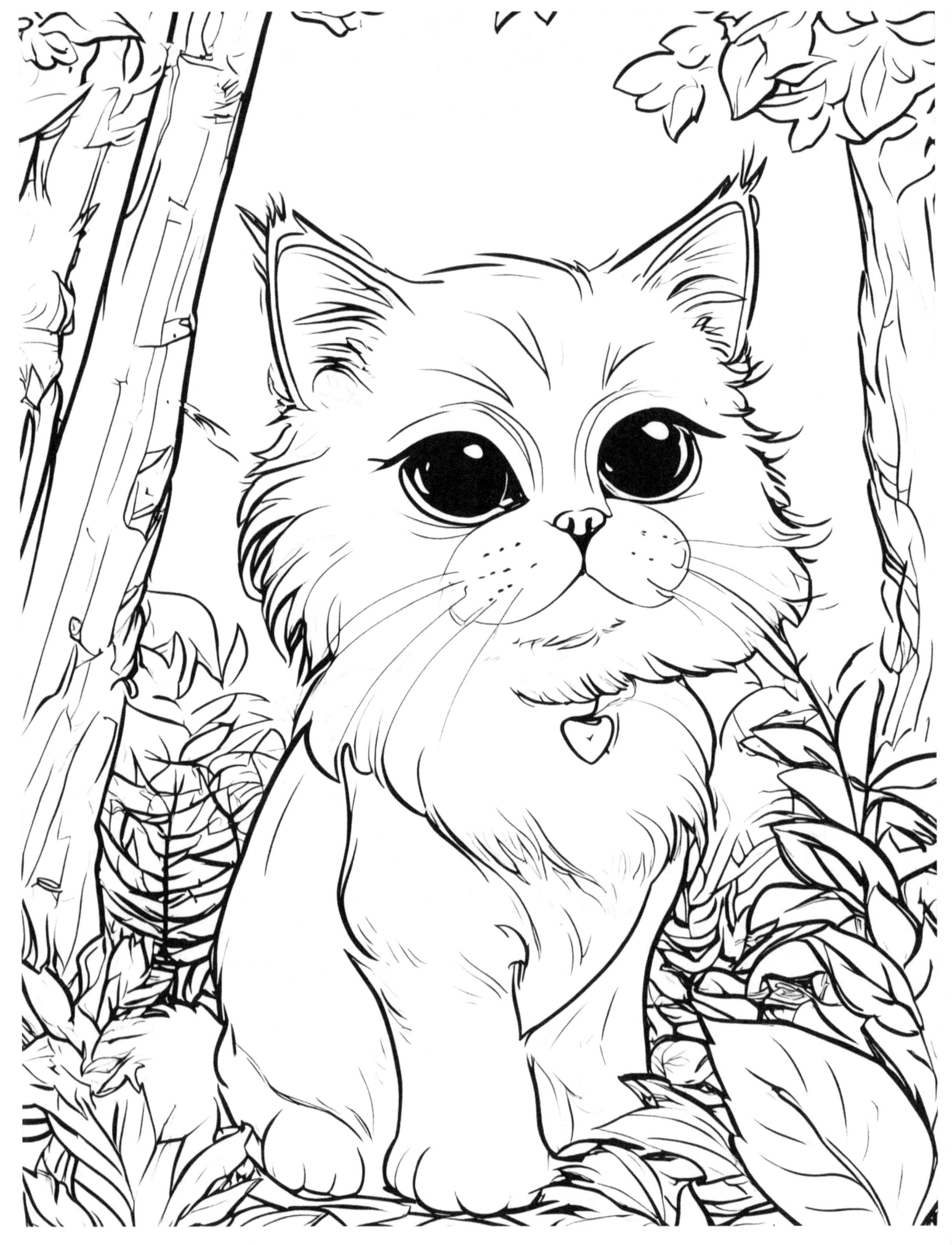

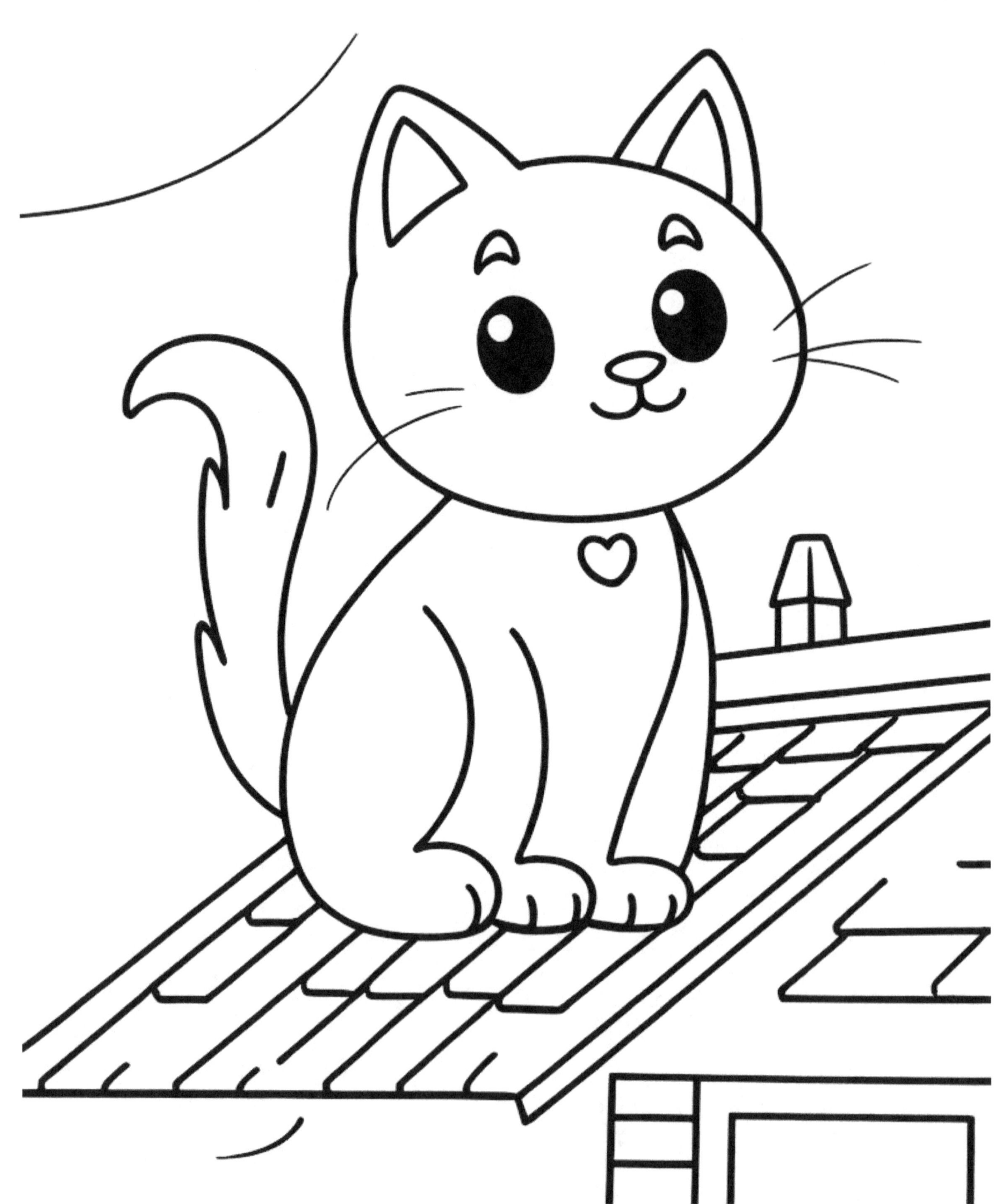

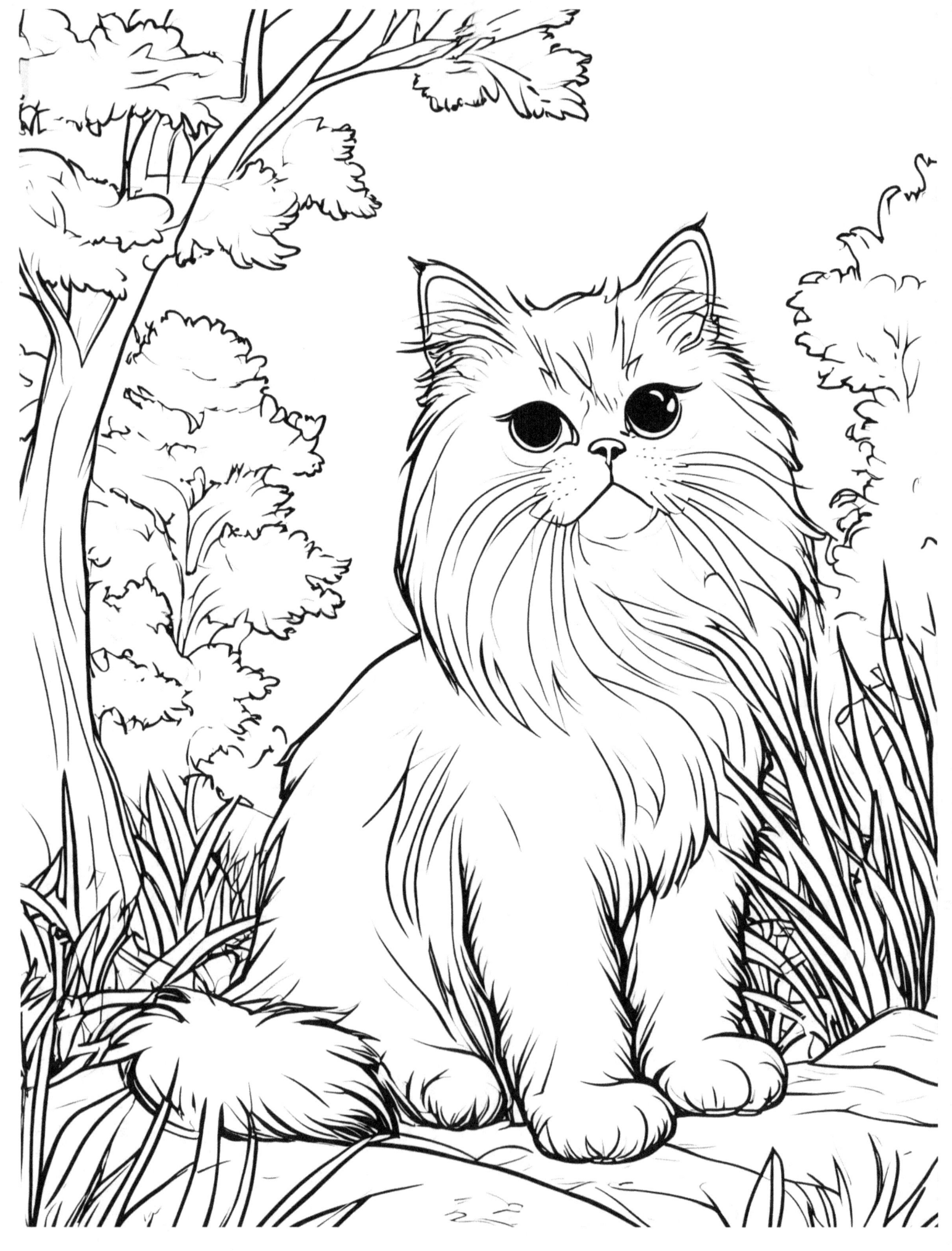

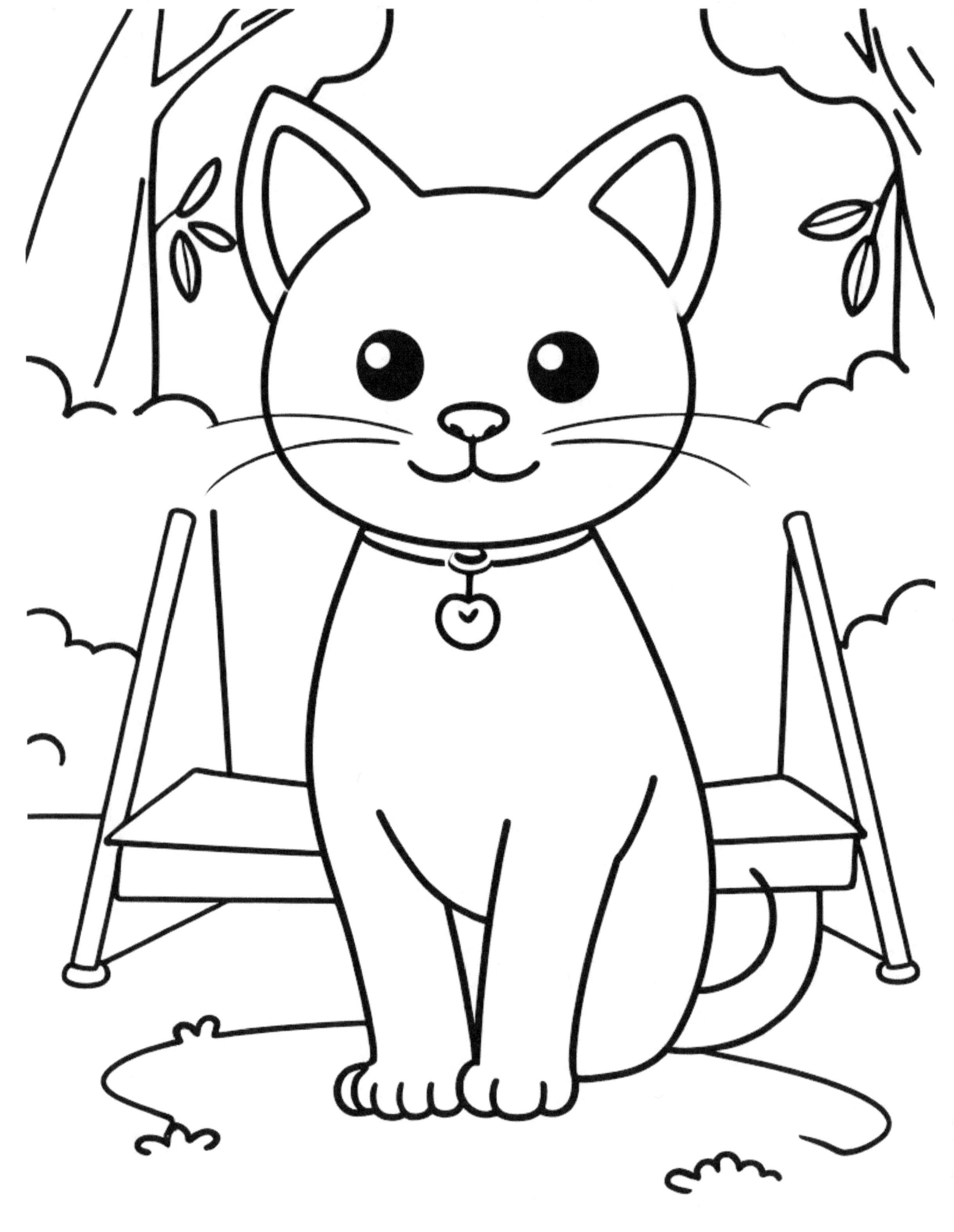

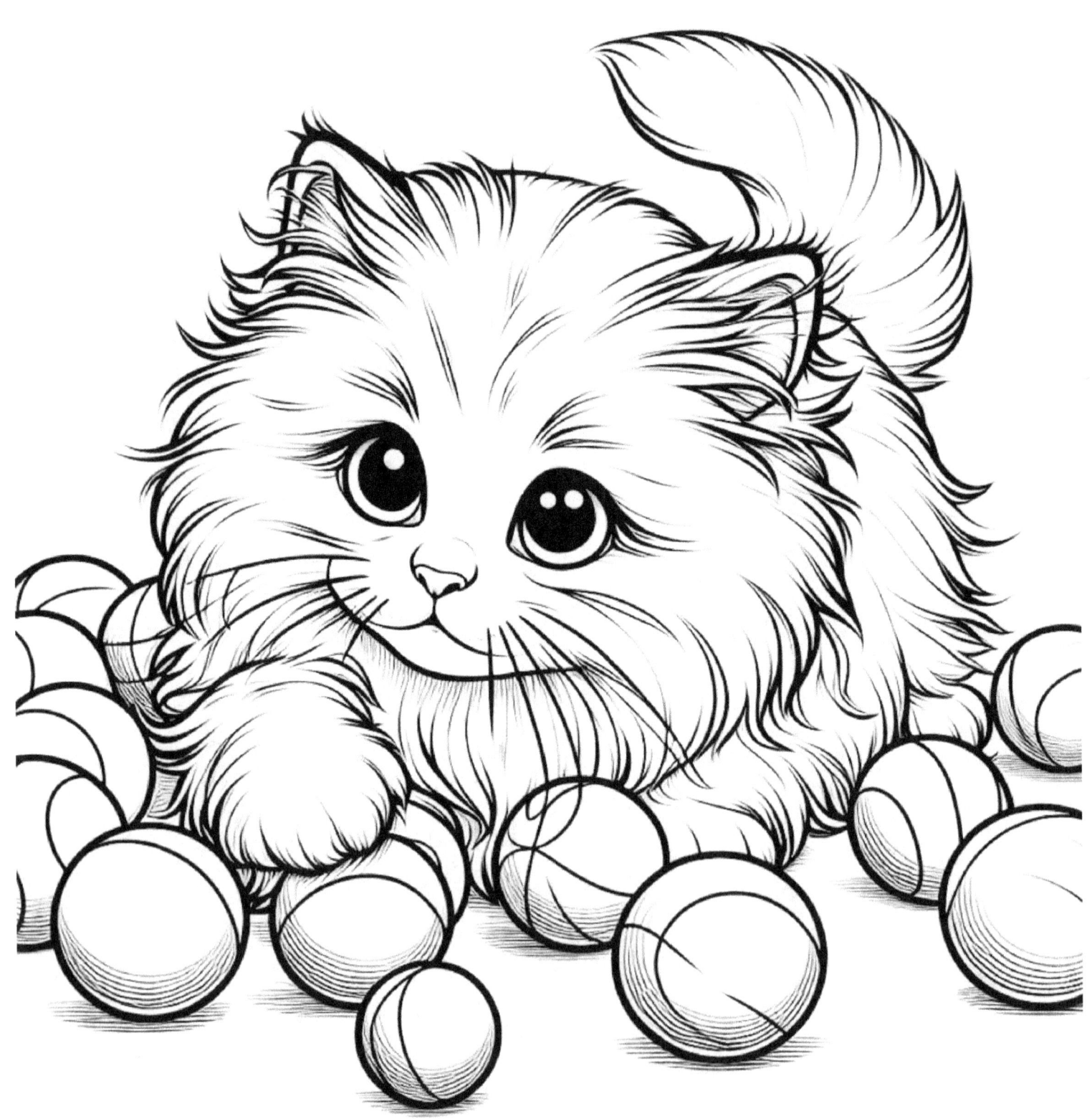

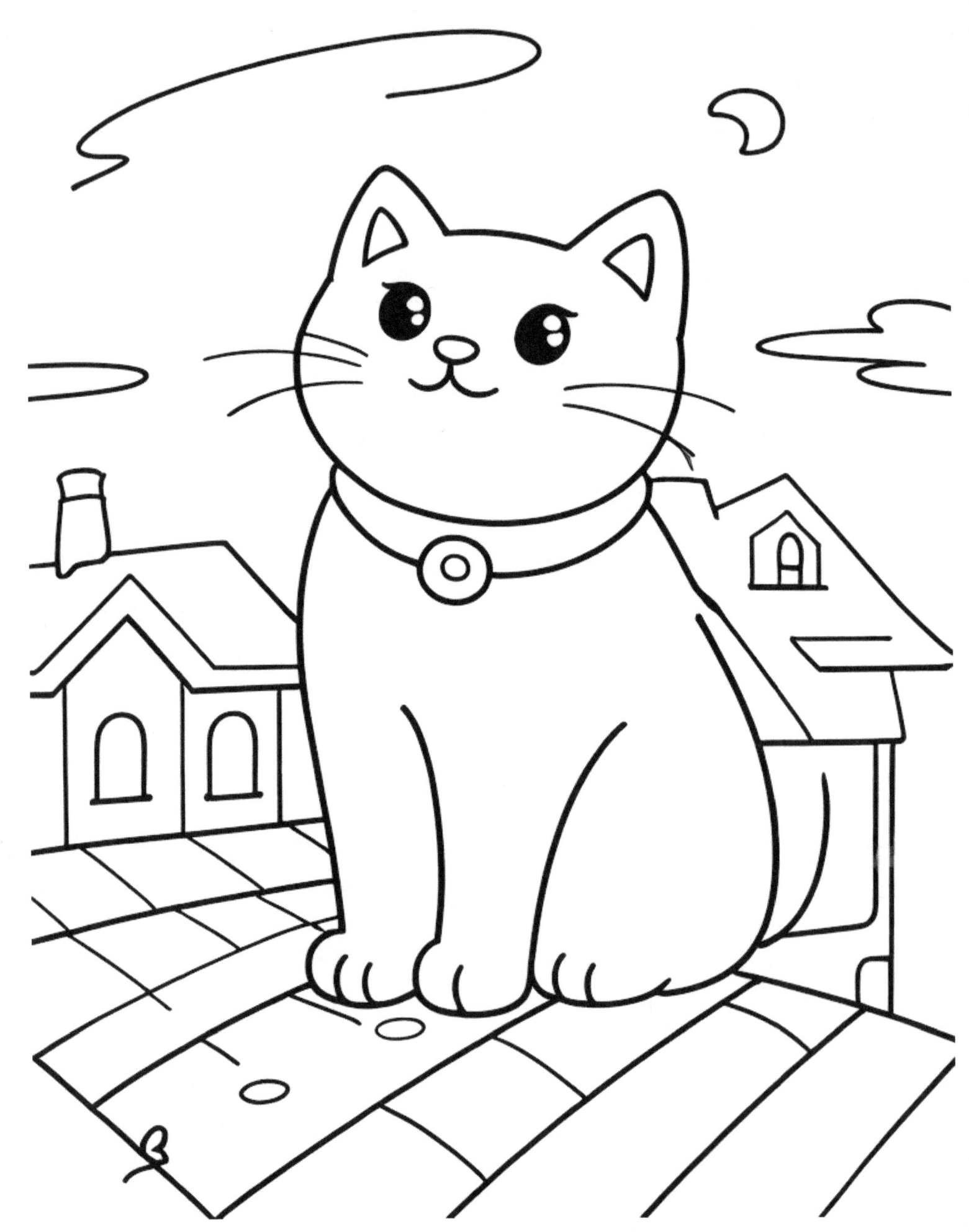

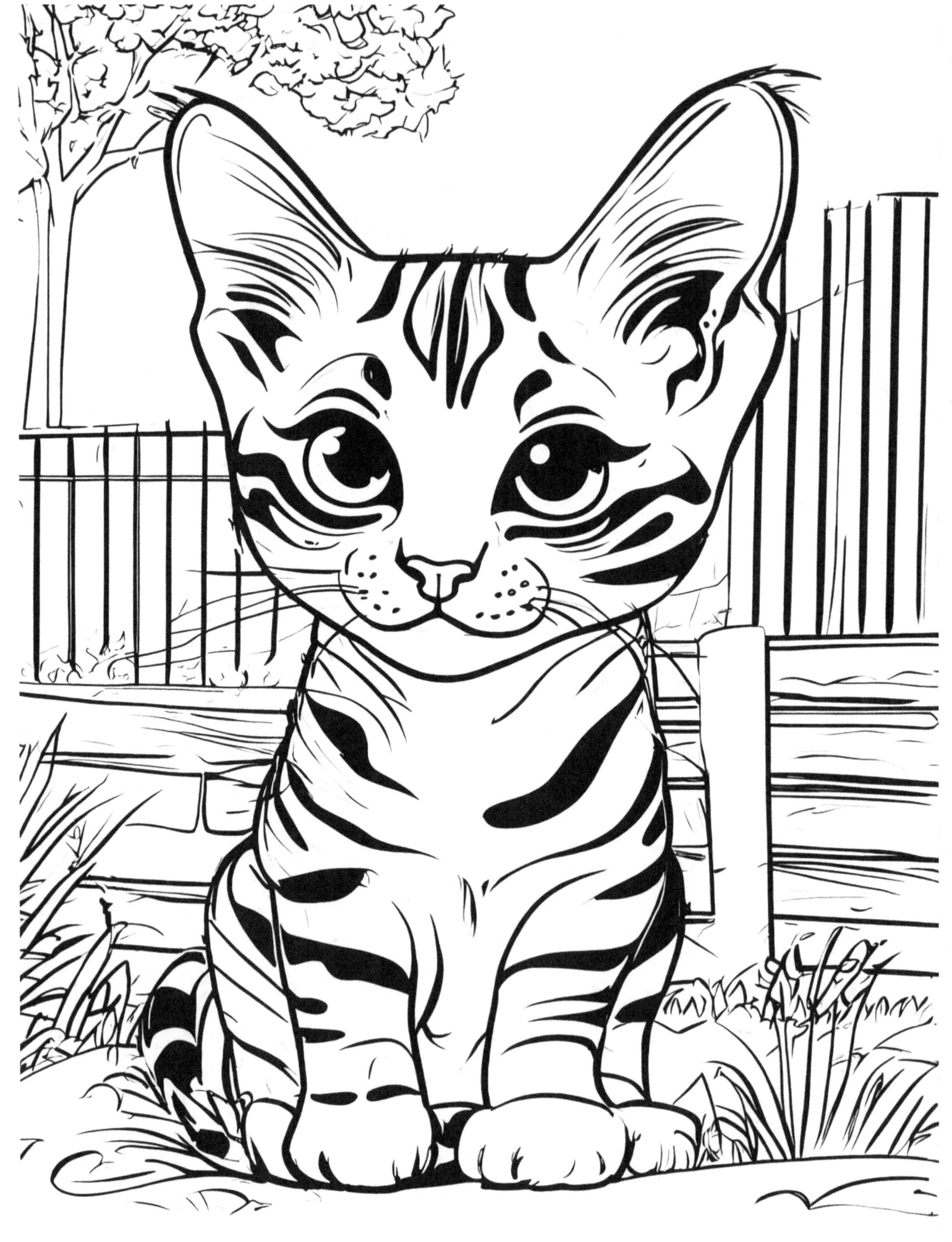

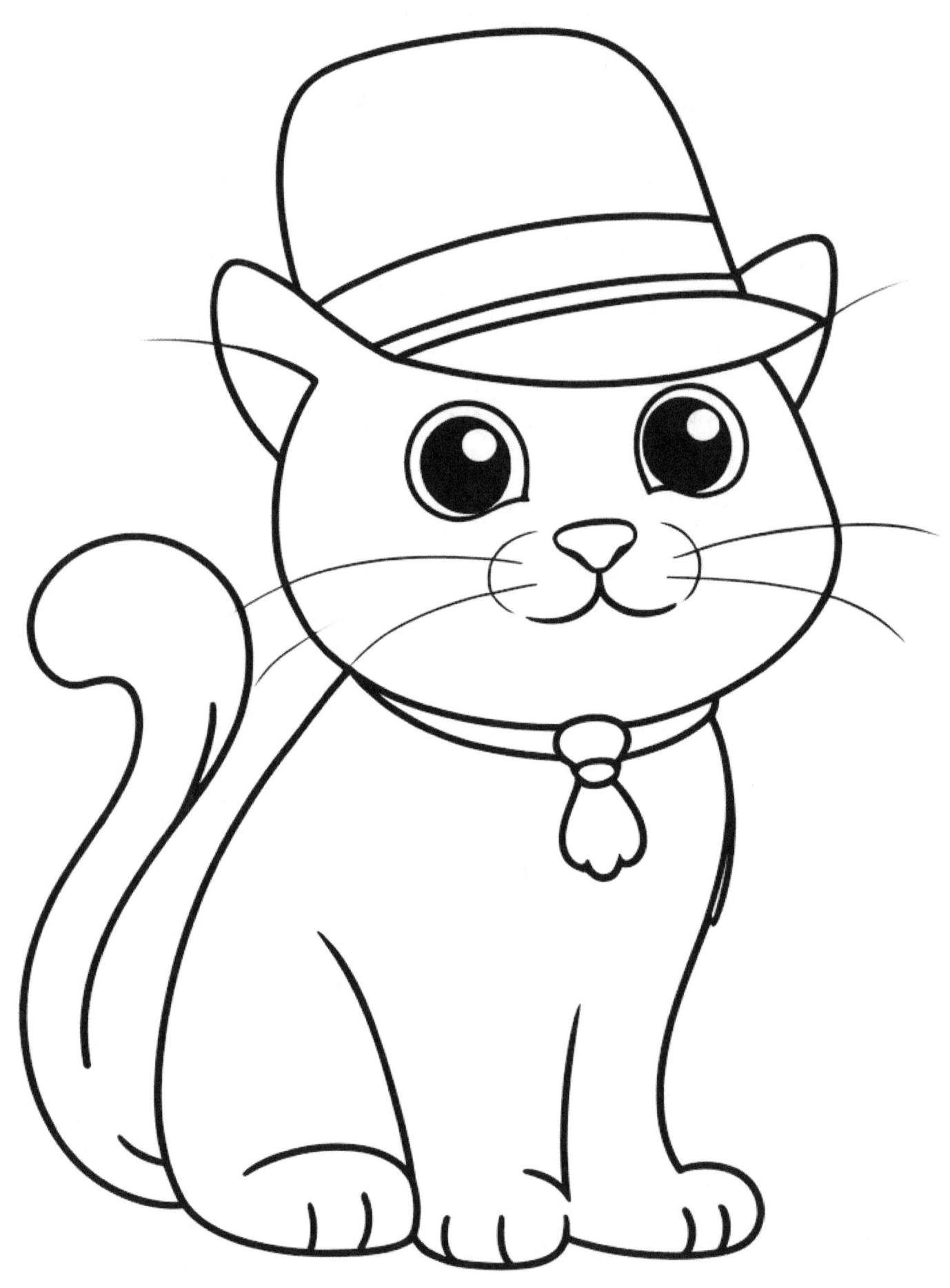

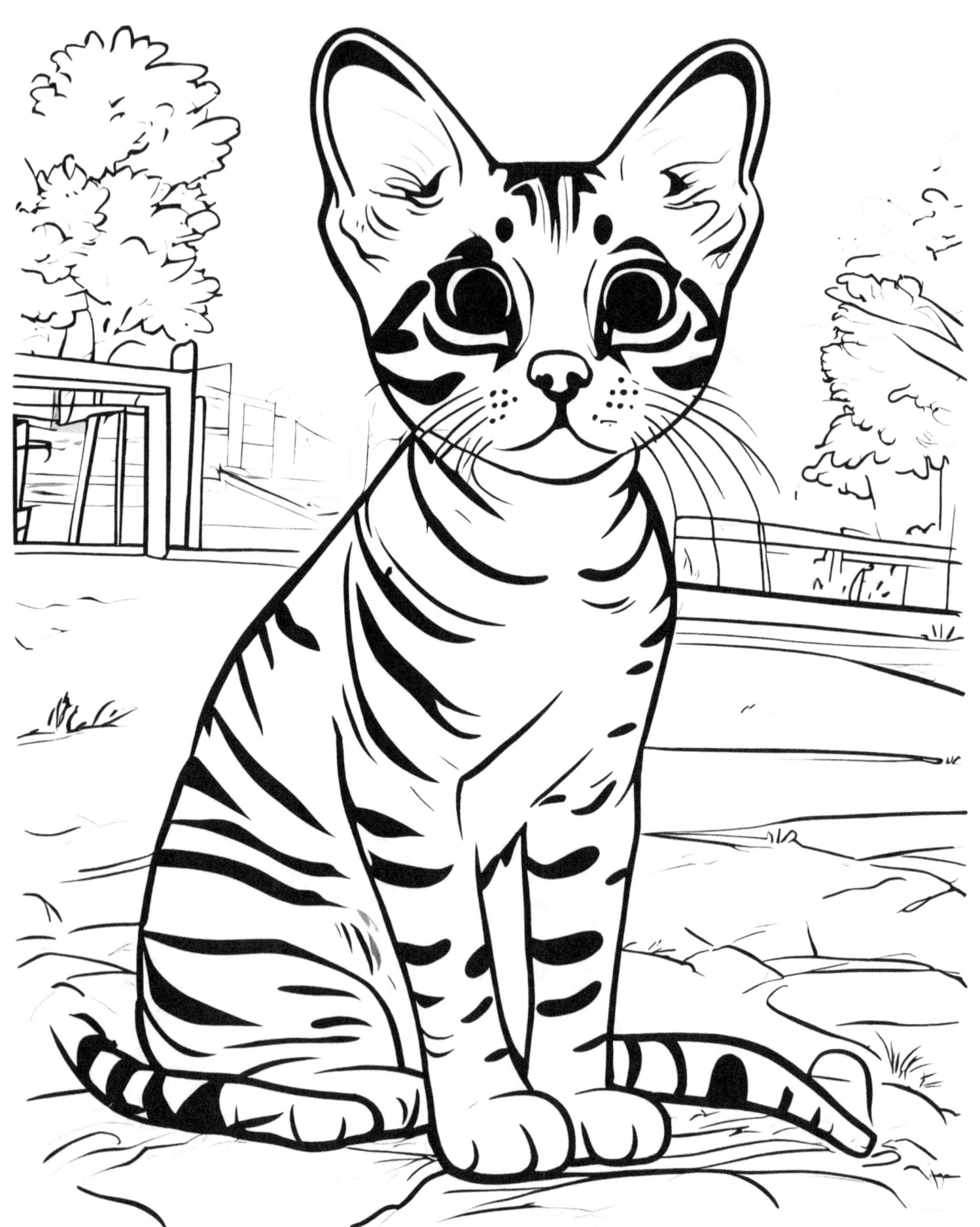

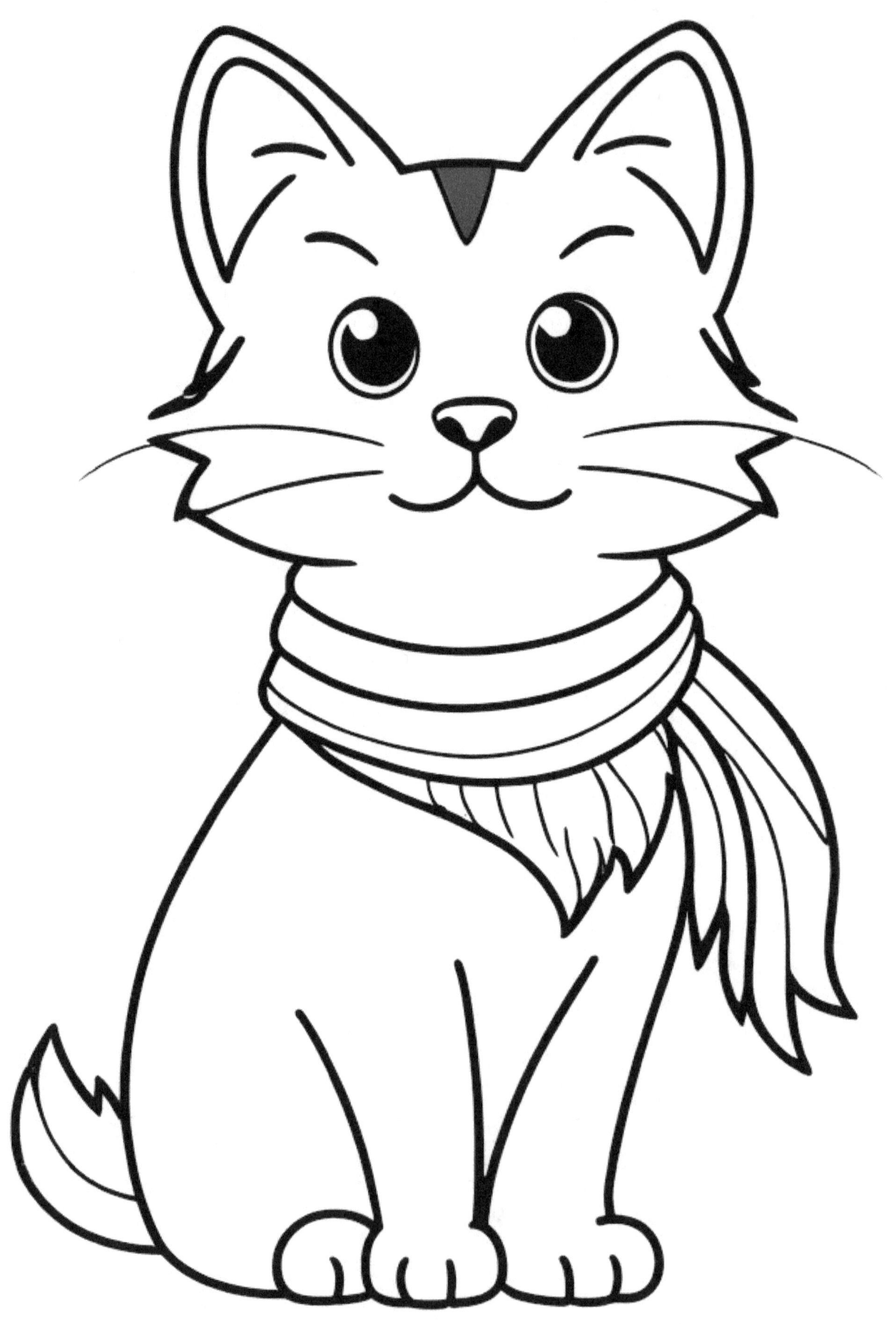

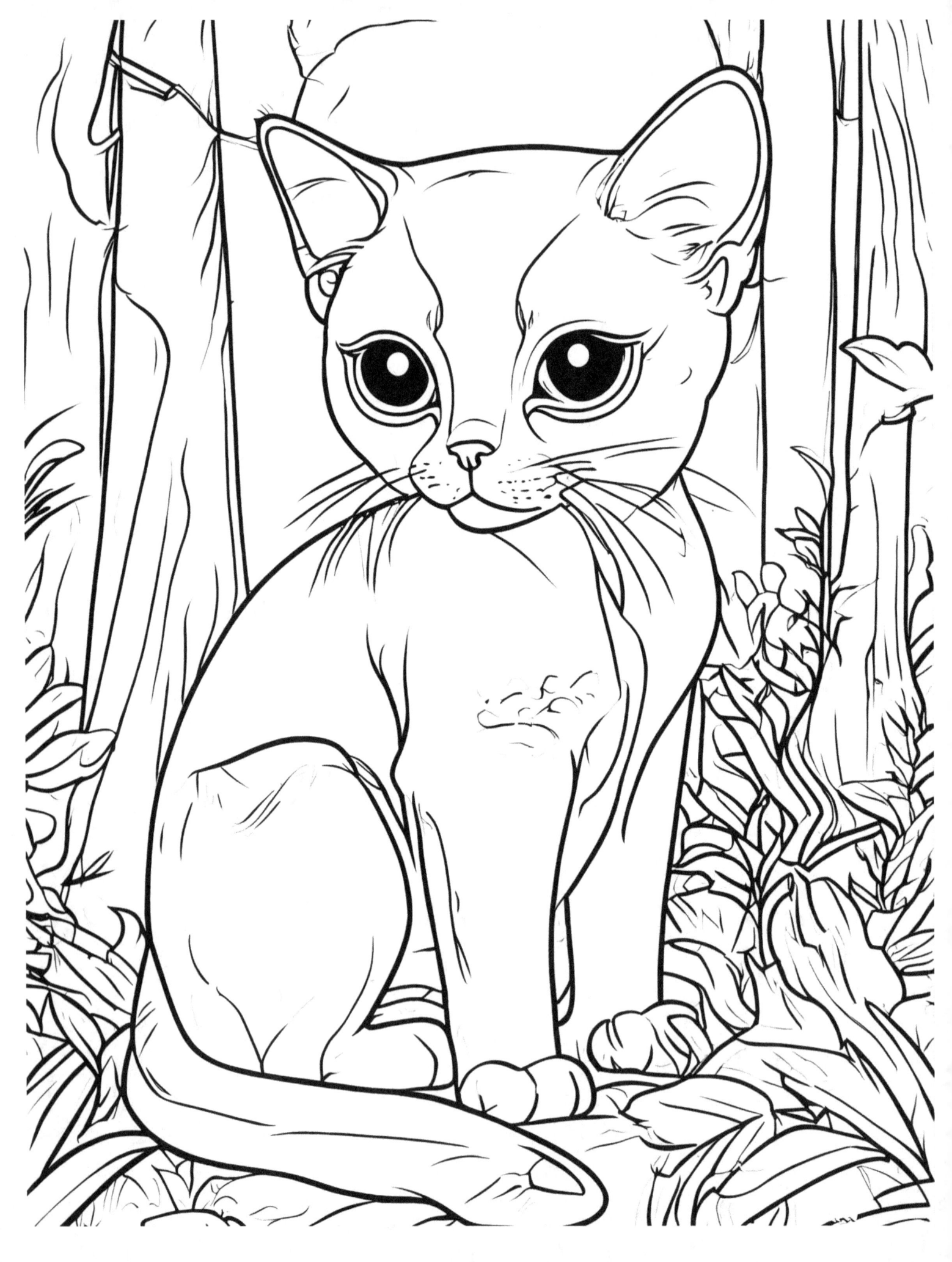

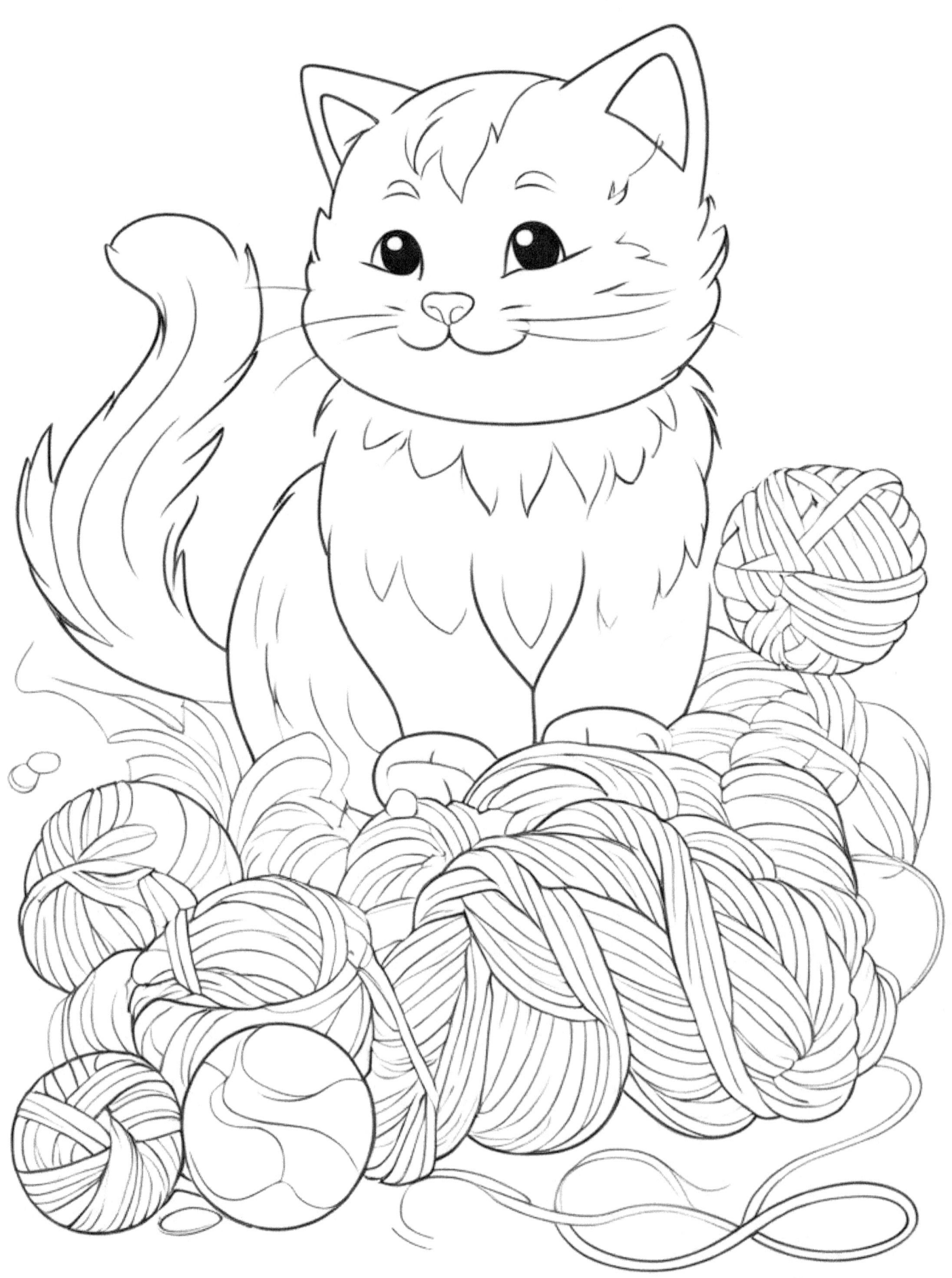

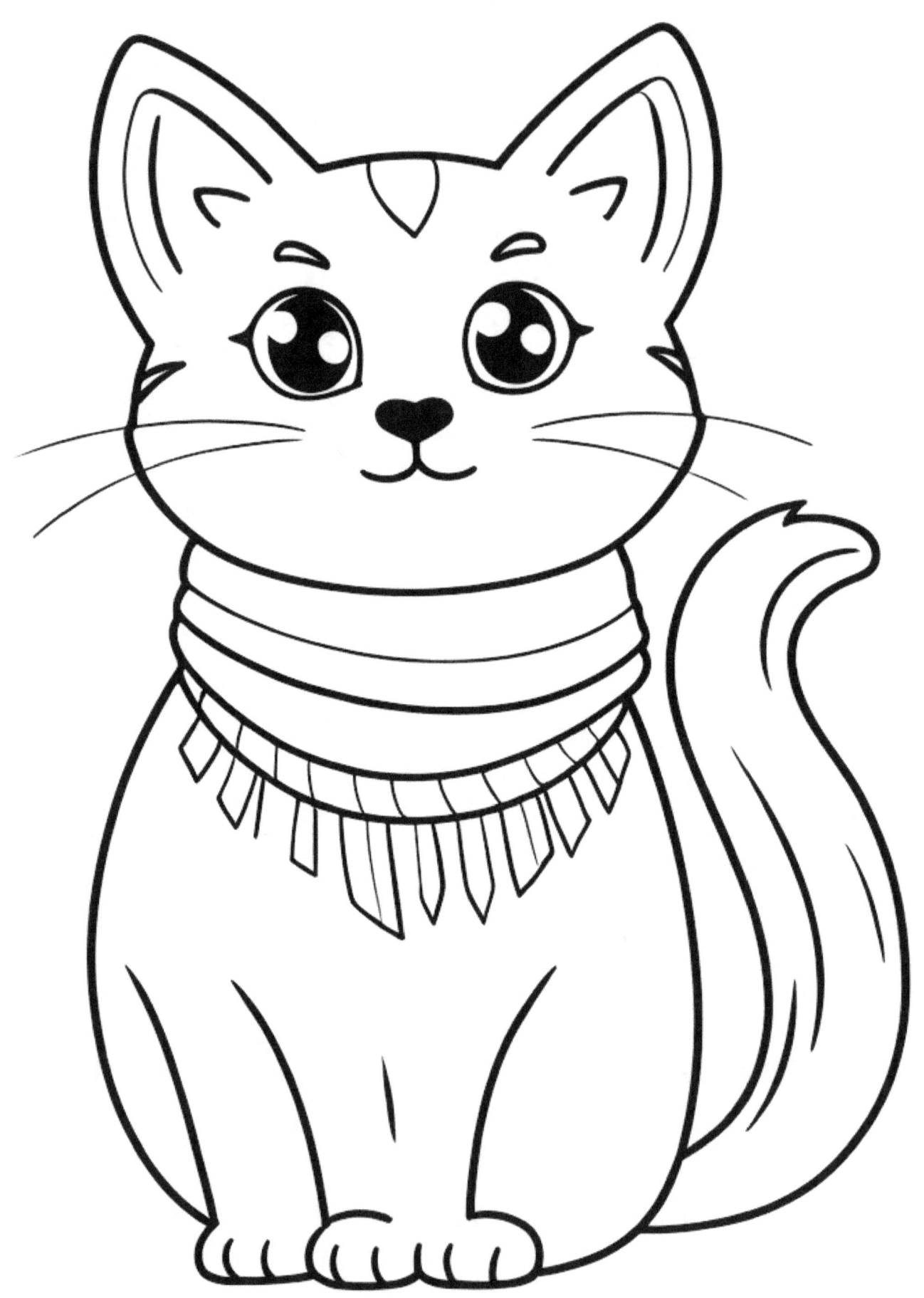

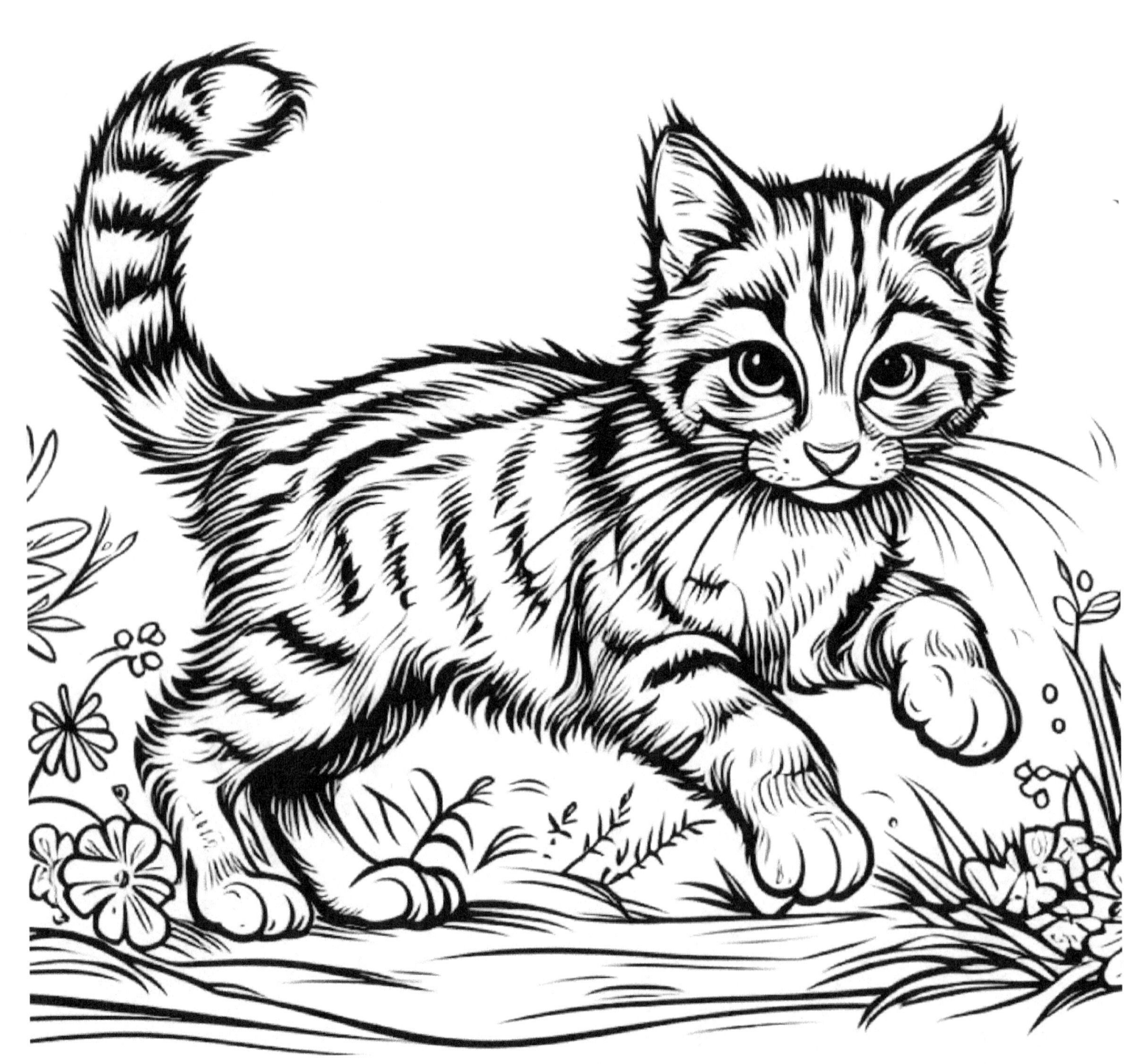

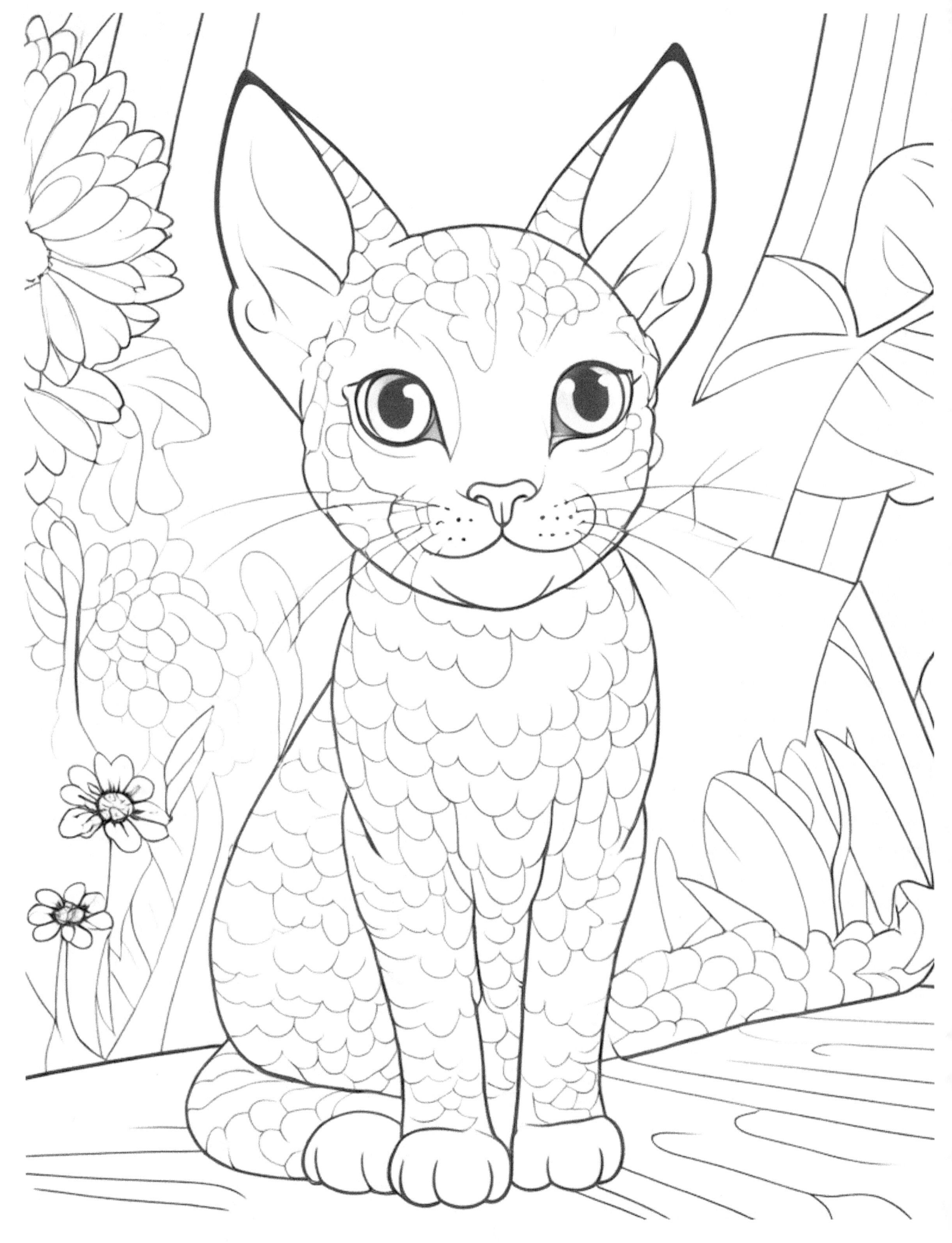

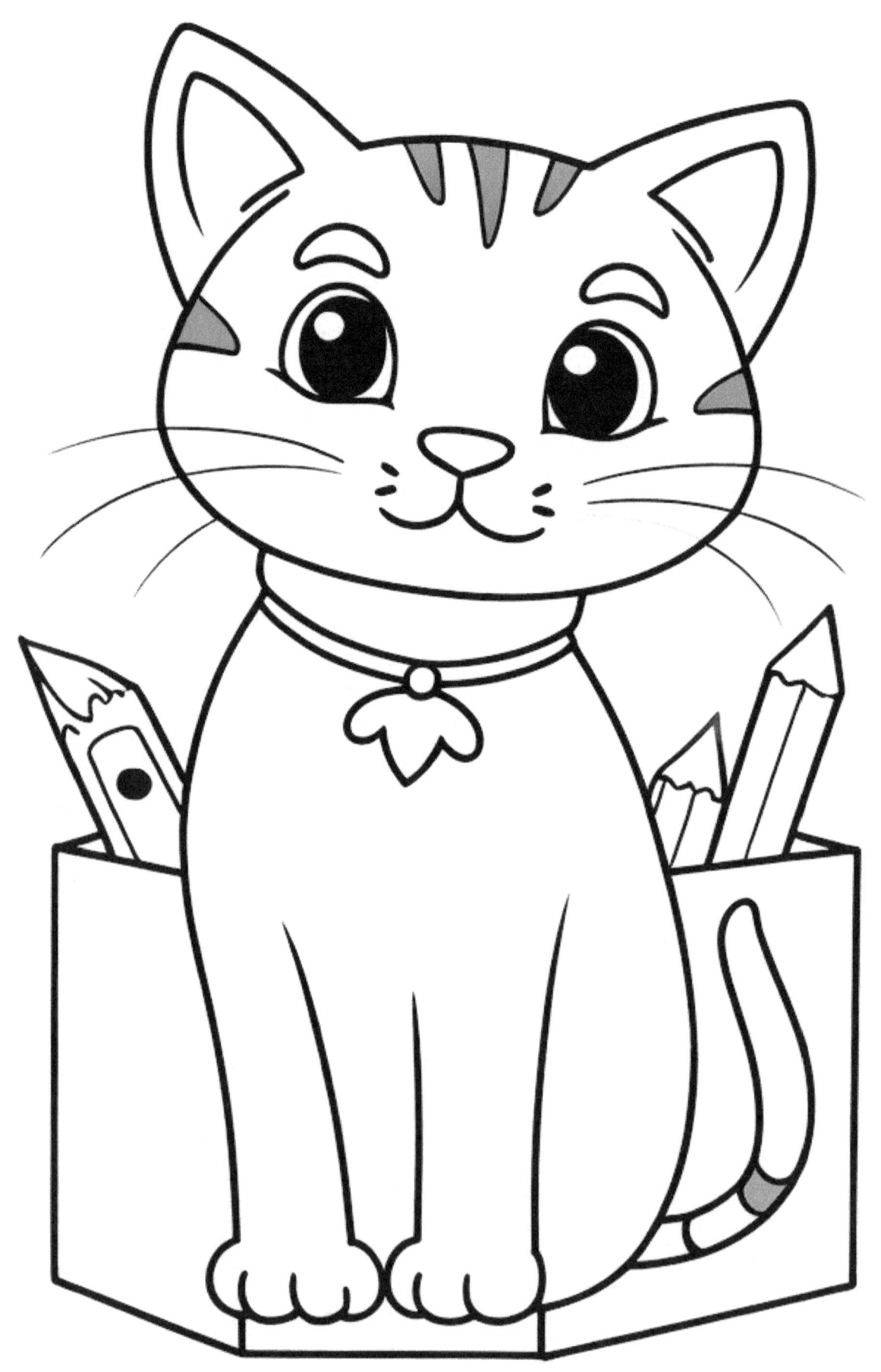

www.ingramcontent.com/pod-product-compliance
Lightning Source LLC
Chambersburg PA
CBHW081019240526
45471CB00017B/3442